THE NEW CATOWNER'S GUIDE

Everything You and Your Cat
Need To Know
About Life in the City

THE NEW YORK CAT OWNER'S GUIDE

Everything You and Your Cat Need To Know About Life in the City

BILL DWORKIN

Cat Editor: Carole C. Wilbourn
With a Word from Morris the Cat
Illustrations by Joy Sikorski

CITY & COMPANY
NEW YORK

City & Company
22 West 23rd Street
New York, NY 10010

Printed in the United States of America

Cover Illustration by Lilla Rogers
Design by Big Duck Studio, NYC

Library of Congress Cataloging-in-Publication Data
available by request

ISBN 1-885492-03-0

Publisher's Note:
Neither City & Company nor the author has any interest,
financial or personal, in the locations listed in this book. No
fees were paid or services rendered in exchange for inclusion
in these pages. Please also note that every effort was made to
ensure the accuracy of all information, including phone
numbers, hours and prices. We suggest that you verify the
costs and reliability of any service you may use.

Acknowledgments

Gratitude for cats shared and cat tales goes to Gene Roth, Louise Fishman, Betsy Crowell, Carol Calhoun, Miranda Bergson, Malachi Bergson, Pat Egan, Lynn Neall, Rochelle Stamboulis, Jenny Snider, Joel Mason, Marilyn Schaefer, Joan and Bernie Crane, Jacky Veneroso and George Strachan. And to the past and present ones, Nicodemus, Natty Bumpo, Black Molly, Chester, Maxie, Captain Paws, Purina, Mouse, Quincy, Cleo, Henry, Dinah, Sweetheart, Al Dente and Tigger.

To my kids themselves, Sylvia and Jake, Boychik and Minnie, Audrey and Lois, who are and have been darling companions. And especially to Gene, who has domesticated us all.

Bill Dworkin

Table of Contents

A WORD FROM MORRIS THE CAT   IX

INTRODUCTION   X

BE PREPARED   1

ACQUIRING A CAT   4

VETERINARIANS   9

KEEPING THE CAT SAFE   25

FURNITURE AND FOOD   29

BEAUTY SALONS   47

CAT BEHAVIORISTS   53

WHEN THE OWNER IS AWAY   57
    Cat Sitters   57
    Veterinary Boarding   61

TRAVEL 65

SPECIAL EVENTS 68

THE CAT AS ART 70

WRITE AWAYS 75

GOOD READING AND VIEWING 79
    Books 79
    Videos 82
    Magazines 83

HAPPY HUNTING GROUNDS 87

ORGANIZATIONS 92

INFO AT YOUR FINGERTIPS 94
    Emergency Numbers 94
    Odds and Ends 95

A Word from Morris The Cat

Having lived seventeen years in Chicago, I know what it's like to live in a big city. As the spokescat for 9-Lives Cat Food, I have lived a rather extravagant lifestyle, travelling exensively throughout the United States and Canada. You're fortunate to live in New York, one of my favorite cities. It's a city that offers everything even the most finicky cats could wish for.

When I'm not busy promoting 9-Lives, my favorite cat food, or travelling nationwide to visit our less fortunate feline friends in animal shelters, I often come to New York to unwind. I urge you to take advantage of all the wonderful things your city has to offer, like visiting your therapist to discuss your owner's less appealing habits, or taking a trip to the beauty salon to let your true "purr-sonality" shine through. Maybe you'd rather stroll over to your psychic to find out what's in store in your next eight lives, or window shop for some unique feline furniture. Whatever your interests, New York has everything a cat could dream of.

To all my finicky New York friends out there, I encourage you to "paws" for a moment and contemplate all the great things your city has to offer. With all of New York's wonderful amenities, it is "cat-egorically" one of the best cities any cool cat could hope to live in.

My "purr-sonal" best to all of you,

Morris

Introduction

You may have noticed that once a cat person finds out that you, too, are a cat lover, your acquaintanceship is off and running. Cat tales are told by even those who are cat-less but once had a cat or knew a cat. A cat has an uncanny way of getting under a person's skin. Once this happens a person is helpless! There's no control over feelings or reason. But more significant, there's no control over the cat. Perhaps it's the

latter that makes the cat such a very splendid creature.
You can't "own" a cat, though at times you may feel that a cat "owns" you. Cats have instinctively mastered the universal mystery of life. They know that their contentment is contageous, and this is reason enough to indulge their whims.

A cat's love is unconditional. No matter how blue your mood, your cat will be there for you. It is this very love that eases and nurtures the psyche of the jangled New Yorker.

My cat, Ziggy-Star-Dust, fills so very many of my needs. Not only does he act as confidant and therapist, but his comic and loving antics light up my life. He is forever teaching me new ways to cope with difficult situations. His late companion, Sonny-Blue, was his mentor and role model, and Star-Dust has picked up several of his habits and talents. "I didn't know that you have a Siamese," people will say after they hear his voice on my message machine. Star-Dust, a big black cat, has adopted Sunny's Siamese voice.

The New York cat person or potential caregiver truly wants to do everything possible to enhance the life of his or her cat, because a happy cat makes a happy person. This concise guide helps to do just that—putting essential information on services, supplies, and practical and unique resources at the caregiver's fingertips.

Carole C. Wilbourn
Cat Therapist
New York City

Be Prepared

The cat is now the favorite companion of animal lovers in the United States. Having overtaken its most celebrated domestic rival, 60,000,000 cats are now inhabiting households nationwide.

There are many reasons why cohabitating with a cat or two in New York City makes a great deal of sense. They don't have to be walked or bathed, and they don't bark or grow to enormous weights. In fact:

1. Cats are usually small and rarely become more than 20 pounds, a plus for apartment living.

2. Cats are quiet, padding about on their soft paws and, unless something disturbs them, not given to crying or wailing.

3. Cats are fastidious and clean themselves constantly.

4. Cats use a litter box or (we've been told) some can even be toilet-trained.

5. Cats can live in the confines of a New York apartment for twenty years without going stark-raving mad.

6. Cats have an insatiable appetite for affection and play.

Of course, cats can also be unpredictable. Consider this list of possible disadvantages before acquiring a cat:

1. They can destroy your furniture and after some years, may even uncover the innards of your upholstery. (This can be avoided to some extent by providing them with adequate alternatives like scratching posts.)

2. The same food they've craved for years can suddenly be refused.

3. They can hide in the most unlikely places and you'll be sure they will never be found (even in a studio apartment).

4. With one leap to a seemingly unreachable shelf, a cat can destroy your most beloved mementos.

5. They may leave cat hair over every surface—bedspreads, pillows, sheets, placemats and clothing.

6. Rugs, precious or practical, may be used for coughing up hair balls.

7. The litter box will have to be changed regularly and scooped daily to avoid noxious odors. (A cat may legitimately avoid a dirty litter box.)

8. Your friends may be allergic to cat hair and will never visit, nor will they bring their asthmatic kids. Or, more seriously, you may be allergic.

Although it may look as though these disadvantages seem to outweigh the advantages, they don't. The tremendous warmth, humor and dependability of a true cat friend will make you a lifetime devotee.

In fact, two cats are usually better than one, both for each other and for their owners. They provide each other with continual company while their owner is away or working; they give twice the pleasure; are twice as entertaining; and two require pretty much the same amount of work as one.

Acquiring a Cat

Cats are everywhere in New York City and, if you want to get one, it's really quite simple. Somehow cats tend to wangle their way into people's lives more readily than the other household pet of choice.

Once you've decided you want a cat, tell your friends and colleagues. It just might be that their cat has or is about to have a litter, or they know one in such a situation. Watch bulletin boards at work, in churches, supermarkets, laundromats, veterinarians' offices and pet shops for photos of cats looking for a home.

Perhaps you'll find an abandoned cat, or one will "just dance down the street into your life," as has actually happened.

There are 330 various breeds of felines and if you are interested in this world of cat fancy, considerable knowledge can be gained from reading source books such as Roger Caras' *Harper Illustrated Handbook of Cats* and *The Readers' Digest Illustrated Book of Cats.* You can also familiarize yourself with the varieties via cat shows, videos, reliable pet shops or breeders whose listings appear in *Cat Fancy* and other magazines.

Most reliable of all, however, are the adoption centers throughout the metropolitan area. They place kittens as well as mature abandoned cats with people they believe will be considerate, caring and responsible. They provide an enormous variety of mixed breeds that are healthy and inexpensive. The following are the main agencies for cat adoption:

ASPCA ADOPTION CENTERS

BRONX
1 Fordham Plaza
Tuesday through Saturday, 11am - 7pm
718-733-0744

BROOKLYN
2336 Linden Blvd.
Tuesday through Saturday, 11am - 7pm
718-272-7200

MANHATTAN
424 East 92nd Street
Seven days, 11am - 7pm
212-876-7700
326 East 110th Street
Tuesday through Saturday, 11am - 7pm
212-722-3620

Acquiring a Cat

QUEENS
92-29 Queens Boulevard
Rego Park
Tuesday through Saturday, 11am - 7pm
718-997-6337

STATEN ISLAND
1490 Richmond Avenue
Tuesday through Saturday, 11am - 7pm
718-370-0679

Rescued kittens and grown cats are available here for adoption. A $45 donation covers adoption, medical examination, initial shots (including rabies), a test for feline leukemia, free spaying or neutering and a carrier for the trip home. You'll need two pieces of identification (one with an address), and before you can leave with any animal the organization speaks with every adult member of your household and checks references. There is a 14-day follow-up examination included in the donation fee. The ASPCA also provides free pet care literature and behavioral counseling.

BIDE-A-WEE
410 East 38th Street, Manhattan
212-532-4455

Last year this organization placed 3,078 cats of all kinds in New York City. A $55 donation covers medical exam, initial shots, neutering or spaying, and tests for feline leukemia,

AIDS and worms. If the cat is over six months old, it has already been spayed or neutered, reducing the required donation to $30. Expect to be interviewed and provide proof of identity and references, including one from your landlord.

HUMANE SOCIETY OF NEW YORK
306 East 59th Street, Manhattan
212-752-4840

Cats of all types and ages are available for adoption here. The application form requires your employer's name, two references, and identification with address. They ask a donation of $50 for short hairs, $60 for long hairs, and $75 for special breeds. Spaying or neutering an adopted kitten costs $25 for a male and $35 for a female. You can also volunteer here, providing extra care for the cats while they're waiting to be adopted.

NORTH SHORE ANIMAL LEAGUE
25 Davis Avenue
Port Washington, Long Island
516-883-7575

A constantly changing and very large selection of older cats and kittens is usually available. You can fill out a request form for special breeds. The voluntary donation covers medical examination, shots, neutering or spaying, a travel kit to get the cat home safely and veterinary care for 30 days. They do a thorough interview, require photo identification, check references, and may visit your home after the adoption to make sure the cat is in good hands.

PLACE FOR CATS
230 East 52nd Street, Manhattan
212-751-2093

These cats are in foster homes. Call for an appointment to see adoptees.

ANIMAL OUTREACH
212-663-1820

Call for an appointment to see adoptee cats in foster homes.

Veterinarians

Ideally your cat's visits to a veterinarian or animal hospital will be only for routine preventative procedures. A strong cat will go through many years of good health without unusual illnesses.

As important as choosing the right cat is choosing the right veterinarian to look after the feline's health. Just as you place your confidence in a physician who provides care for your own well being, your trust in a vet should be equally as secure.

Your cat is being entrusted to the world of animal medicine, and the vet must act as your cat's interpreter. The vet should make your cat as comfortable as possible so that examination and treatment are accepted without antagonism. You should be able to tell within the first meeting whether or not the skilled hands of a compassionate vet are putting your cat at ease.

An efficiently run veterinarian's office will keep you informed of your cat's periodic needs and when its precautionary shots are due. The staff and the order, odor and cleanliness of the vet's premises are good indicators of the level of quality and professionalism you can expect.

Veterinarians

Veterinarian offices are found in most neighborhoods throughout the city. Most likely friends or neighbors will share their recommendations, but be sure to check out all referrals before making your decision. Also consider your proximity to the veterinarian's office since transportation may not always be available or friendly when you need it.

Some veterinarians make house visits, but mostly to senior citizens or house-bound owners. If this is important to you, it is suggested that you call to confirm. Emergency phone numbers are, however, usually available for non-office hours.

The largest resource for veterinarian services in New York is the Animal Medical Center, 510 East 62nd Street, (212) 838-8100, which is open 24 hours a day, every day of the year.

In New York all veterinarians treat cats, although only the two below make a specialty of feline medicine.

THE CAT PRACTICE
137 Fifth Avenue
212-677-1401

This clinic was founded in 1973 by Dr. Paul Rowan and Carole C. Wilbourn. Sold in 1978, it is now owned and operated by veterinarian William "Skip" Sullivan, who provides shots, treatment and surgery, boarding and adoption. This vet placed 300 cats for adoption in the last year alone. Appointments only, seven days a week.

FELINE HEALTH CENTER
1533 First Avenue
212-879-0700

There are three vets participating here. By appointment only, seven days a week, with 24 hour emergency service.

The following is a selection of veterinarians and animal hospitals throughout the city. (Animal hospitals are often group practices with extensive facilities.)

WEST SIDE

WEST VILLAGE VETERINARY HOSPITAL
705 Washington Street
212-691-1805
M,T,Th 8:30-6:30; W,F,Sa 9-1

ABINGDON SQUARE VETERINARY CLINIC
107 Greenwich Avenue
212-242-9169
M-Sa 10-12:30; 5-6:30

PETMINDERS ANIMAL HOSPITAL
158 Duane Street
212-406-0970
M,W,F 9-5; T,Th 10-7:30; Sa 10-5

Veterinarians

ANIMAL CLINIC OF GREENWICH VILLAGE
257 W. 18th Street
212-924-8866
M,T,Th 10-7; Sa 10-4

CHELSEA DOG AND CAT HOSPITAL
303 W. 20th Street
212-929-6963
M-F 9-5; Sa 9-2

ANIMAL HOSPITAL OF CHELSEA
164 W. 21st Street
212-243-3020
M,W,F 9-5; T,Th 9-7; Sa 9-1

RICHARD NOVICK
267 W. 25th Street
212-691-9270
M,T,Th,F 10-12, 4:30-6
W,Sa 10-12, 5-6; Su 11-12

CLINTON VETERINARY CENTER
357 W. 52nd Street
212-333-5548
M,W,F 9-5; T,Th 9-7; Sa 9-3

ANSONIA VETERINARY CENTER
207 W. 75th Street
212-496-2100
M,T,W,F 8:30-6:30; Th 8:30-7:30; Sa 8:30-4; Su 10-1
24-hour patient care available.

RIVERSIDE VETERINARY GROUP
219 W. 79th Street
212-787-1993
M,W,Th,F 9-7; T 9-8; Sa 9-5

WESTSIDE VETERINARY CENTER
220 W. 83rd Street
212-580-1800
M-Th 10-8:30; F 10-5:30; Sa, Su 10-4:30
24-hour on-call emergency service for established clients;
24-hour patient care available.

ANIMAL GENERAL
558 Columbus Avenue
212-501-9600
M,F 9-6; T,W,Th 9-7; Sa 9-3
24-hour on-call emergency service for established clients;
24-hour patient care available; house calls by appointment.

Veterinarians

COLE ANIMAL HOSPITAL
230 W. 97th Street
212-222-6664
M,T,W,F 9-6; Sa 9-1

RIVERSIDE ANIMAL HOSPITAL
250 W. 100th Street
212-865-2224
M 9-9; T,W,F 10-7; Th 3-9; Sa 10-5; Su 11-3

COLUMBIA ANIMAL HOSPITAL
229 W. 101st Street
212-864-1144
Daily 9-5; Su - By appointment

CATHEDRAL DOG & CAT HOSPITAL
250 W. 108th Street
212-864-3631
M,T,F 10-6; Th 10-8; Sa 10-2

145TH STREET ANIMAL HOSPITAL
454 W. 145th Street
212-234-3489
M,T,F 9-6; Th 9-6; Sa 9-1

CABRINI VETERINARY HOSPITAL
839 W. 181st Street
212-740-3819
M,T,Th,F 9-6; W 9-11; Sa 9-12

EAST SIDE

EAST VILLAGE VETERINARIANS
241 Eldridge Street
212-674-8640
M,T,F 9-5:30; W 9-3; Th 10-7; Sa 10-2

TRIBECA-SOHO ANIMAL HOSPITAL
281 W. Broadway
212-925-6100
M-Th 8-7; F 8-6; Sa 8-5

ST. MARKS VETERINARY HOSPITAL
348 E. 9th Street
212-477-2688
M-F 9-7; Sa, Su 9-4
24-hour on-call emergency service and house calls.

Veterinarians

WASHINGTON SQUARE ANIMAL HOSPITAL
23 E. 9th Street
212-674-1670
M-F 9-6; Sa 9-3
Available for house calls.

THE VILLAGE VETERINARIAN
204 E. 10th Street
212-979-9870
M-Th 8-6; F 8-3

MURRAY HILL ANIMAL HOSPITAL
47 E. 30th Street
212-685-2857
M,T,Th,F 8-6; W 8-3; Sa 9-4

MIDTOWN ANIMAL HOSPITAL
240 E. 33rd Street
212-683-0309
M-F 8:30-7; Sa 9-1:30

EAST BAY ANIMAL CLINIC
612 Second Avenue
212-481-7999
M,W,F 9-12, 3:30-6; T,Th 3:30-8:00; Sa 9-1; Su 10-3

RIVERGATE VETERINARY CLINIC
649 Second Avenue

212-213-9885
M,W,F 8-6; T,Th 8-8; Sa 9-3

BIDE-A-WEE VETERINARY CLINIC
410 E. 38th Street
212-532-5884
M,T,W,F 9-4; Th 9-8; Sa 9-2

LEXINGTON VETERINARIAN GROUP
133 E. 39th Street
212-889-7778
M,T,W 9-5:30; Th 9-7:30; Sa 9-12:30

EAST SIDE ANIMAL HOSPITAL
321 E. 52nd Street
212-751-5176
M-F 8-7; Sa 8-2

NEW YORK VETERINARY HOSPITAL
301 E. 55th Street
212-355-5490
M-F 10-7; Sa 9-1; Su 9-1

HUMANE SOCIETY OF NEW YORK
306 E. 59th Street
212-752-4840
M-F, Su 9-12, 1-3:30; Sa 9-2

Veterinarians

ANIMAL MEDICAL CENTER
510 E. 62nd Street
212-838-8100
24 hours a day

PARK EAST ANIMAL HOSPITAL
52 E. 64th Street
212-832-8417
M-Su 8-6
24-hour on-call emergency service for established clients;
24-hour patient care available; house calls by appointment.

UNIVERSITY ANIMAL HOSPITAL
354 E. 66th Street
212-288-8884
M-F 8-8; Sa 9-1; Sa 9-4

CENTER FOR VETERINARY CARE
236 E. 75th Street
212-734-7480
M,F 9-5:30; T,W,Th 9-6:30; Sa 9-3
24-hour on-call emergency service for established clients;
24-hour patient care available.

DR. THOMAS DE VINCENTIS
430 E. 75th Street
535-3250
M-F 8-12 & 3-6; Sa 9-2

24-hour on-call emergency service for established clients; house calls by appointment.

LENOX HILL VETERINARIANS
204 E. 76th Street
212-879-1320
M,W,F 9-6; T,Th 9-7:30; Sa 9-1

MANHATTAN VETERINARY GROUP LTD.
240 E. 80th Street
212-988-1000
M-F 8-4; Sa, Su 9-5

DR. LEE KEATING
1435 Lexington Avenue
876-8253
Tu-Sa 10-6, Th evenings by appointment

MERCY VETERINARY HOSPITAL
134 E. 82nd Street
212-861-5601
M,W,F 8:30-5; T,Th 8:30-8:00; Sa 10-4

Veterinarians

YORKVILLE ANIMAL HOSPITAL
227 E. 84th Street
212-249-8802
M-F 9-6; Sa 9-2

ANIMAL CLINIC OF NEW YORK
1623 First Avenue
212-628-5580
M-Th 8:30-7; F 8-5; Sa 8:30-1

CARNEGIE HILL VETERINARIANS
201 E. 89th Street
212-369-5665
M,T,Th 9-12 and 4:30-7; W,F 9-12; Sa 10-1

ASPCA
422 E. 92nd Street
212-876-7700
M-F 9-7; Sa 8:30-3

EAST HARLEM VETERINARY CLINIC
2296 First Avenue
212-348-8314
M,F 10-6; T,Th 1-9; W 1-6; Sa 11-5

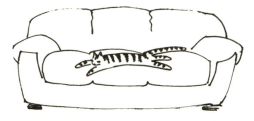

BRONX

BENDER ANIMAL HOSPITAL
6118 Riverdale Avenue
718-549-8131
M-F 9:15-11:30; 4:00-5:30; Sa 9:15-12:30

BROADWAY ANIMAL HOSPITAL OF RIVERDALE
5664 Broadway
718-543-5600
M,W,F 9:30-11, 3:30-6; T,Th 9:30-12; Sa 9:30-1:30

TRIBORO VETERINARY HOSPITAL
604 Grand Concourse
718-292-1770
M-F 10-2 and 4-6:30; Sa 9:30-2

QUEENS

ANIMAL HOSPITAL OF THE ROCKAWAYS
114-10 Beach Channel Drive
718-474-0500
M,T, Th 10-12, 2-4, 7-8; Wed 10-12; Fr 2-4; Sa, Su 10-12

BELLEROSE ANIMAL HOSPITAL
24201 Jamaica Avenue
718-347-1057
M-F 9-8; Sa 9-3:30; Su 9-11:30

Veterinarians

FOREST HILLS CAT HOSPITAL
69-02 Austin Street
718-520-1111
M-Th 9:30-12 & 4-8; Fri 9:30-12 & 4-6; Sa 9-3, Su 9-1:30

LAURENCE ANIMAL HOSPITAL
77-23 Queens Blvd., Elmhurst
718-458-0500
M 10-2 and 4-6:30; T,Th 10-6; W,F,Sa 10-3

BROOKLYN

ANIMAL CLINIC OF SUNSET PARK
5908 5th Avenue
718-492-9090
M, T, Th, Fr 10:30-7; Sa 10:30-3

BAYRIDGE ANIMAL CLINIC
689 86th Street
718-833-0700
M-F 10-12 & 2-4 & 5-7:30, Sat 10-12 & 2-4; Su 11-1

COBBLE HILL ANIMAL HOSPITAL
181 Court Street
718-834-1800
M, Tu, W 10-1 & 5-7; Fr, Sa 10-1; closed Th and Su

Veterinarians

MOBILE VETERINARY UNIT
94 Avenue U
718-373-0240

PET HAVEN ANIMAL HOSPITAL
290 McDonald Avenue
718-435-6900
M-Th 10-1 and 4-8; F 10-7; Su 10-1

PARK SLOPE ANIMAL KIND VETERINARY HOSPITAL
408 Seventh Avenue
718-832-3899
M-F 7-12 and 5-7; Sa 9:30-5; Su 10-4

STATEN ISLAND

ALL PETS ANIMAL HOSPITAL
277 Van Duzer Street
718-442-1117
M-Th 10:30-8:00; F 10-7; Sa 10-2:30

SALEM SMALL ANIMAL HOSPITAL
1409 Richmond Avenue
718-370-0700
M-F 10-8; Sa 10-2

Veterinarians

SPECIFICALLY HOUSE CALLS

DOWNTOWN VETERINARY HOUSE CALLS
295 Greenwich Avenue
212-619-9119

A HOUSE CALL FOR PETS
240 W. 10th Street
212-989-6651

DR. GEORGE M. KORIN
212-838-2569

DR. MICHAEL BRODSKY
914-738-5014

DR. AMY J. ATTAS
212-581-PETS

Keeping the Cat Safe

While cats are remarkably resilient and can recover amazingly well from traumas of all sorts, no one has yet documented their nine lives! In fact, the miraculous survival of a cat who falls thirty stories is rare compared to the number who succumb to high-rise syndrome.

Keep a watchful eye on the following sources of potential catastrophe and keep a list of emergency numbers by the phone.

1. **Open Windows**. Always make certain windows are screened securely to prevent cats from wandering out on ledges, probably the most lethal place for a cat in New York City.

2. **Household Appliances**. Washing machines and dryers should always be checked for the inquisitive cat who has decided to investigate the inside of the machine. The sharp blades of a fan or heat from your toaster can hurt your cat. Cat-proof your electrical cords and cover any unused outlets. Also, check your oven before every use.

3. **Needles and Thread, etc.** Cats consider thread and string as their most natural playthings, and will swallow them, needle and all. Dental floss, yarn and dangling drapery cords can also be hazardous.

4. **Plants.** Cats like eating greens, but certain house plants are dangerous to animals. Watch for philodendrons, diefenbachia, English ivy and caladium. Consult your vet, poison control center, or library for a complete, updated list of poisonous plants.

5. **Locked Closets.** When you leave your home, say goodbye in person to make sure your cat is not locked away in a closed closet or drawer.

6. **Dehydration.** Always keep a bowl of fresh water available so that your cat can drink his fill. Distilled bottled or filtered water is easier on cats' kidneys because of low mineral deposits.

7. **Access to Litter Box.** For your cat's comfort and your own, make certain the room with the litter box is *always* accessible.

8. **Insecticides.** Rat poison can kill a cat. Make sure insecticides are not sprayed where cats dwell or have access. When necessary, consult a cat-friendly exterminator. Also, cleaning fluids should be kept out of reach.

9. **Dogs**. Cats can live in harmony or armed truce with a familiar dog. But watch out for the intrusion of a foreign canine. Fur (and more) can fly and so will your cat's well-being.

10. **Children** sometimes can unknowingly be rough on pets. Be sure very young children play with your cat under adult supervision.

11. **Chicken and Other Bones**. Do not leave these about for cats to chew or swallow. They can be fatal.

12. **Rubber Bands and Paper Clips**. These can be swallowed by a cat with dangerous results. A cat can also get its claws painfully caught in rubber bands left on door knobs.

13. **Tinfoil, corks, and cellophane** can be ingested and cause an intestinal blockage.

14. **Sharp objects** such as scissors, knives, safety pins, push pins, razor blades, etc. should be stored out of paw's reach.

15. **Medicine** should be kept out of your cat's reach. Consult your veterinarian if your cat has ingested any human medicine accidentally. Never administer any "home remedies."

16. **Antifreeze**. Most antifreeze contains a sweet-tasting ingredient called ethylene glycol. Its taste and scent are

attractive but fatal if ingested. Wood alcohol is also an ingredient in many household products and is equally poisonous.

17. **Garbage Cans.** Your garbage container should be securely covered so your cat doesn't wreak havoc with its contents. Beware of overturned wastebaskets.

18. **Many cat toys** can be hazardous. Check the toy for sturdiness before buying.

19. **Brooms** should be stored in a cat-proof spot. Chewing on broom straws can cause your cat to choke and can result in body perforation.

20. **Shopping Bag Handles.** Remove the handles from shopping bags so your cat's head doesn't become entangled in the handles. Such an incident can cause residual anxiety for a cat and cat's companion.

21. **Pantyhose**. It is not uncommon for a cat to ingest nylon hose or other fabrics they find interesting.

Furniture and Food

To make cats at home in human surroundings, provide them with creature comforts they can call their own. There are a few basic items that are musts for any cat household: the litter box and scooper, one or more scratching posts, a dish (preferably not plastic), a bed, a carrier and, of course, food and water. Beyond the necessities, the varieties of home furnishings available include a few extraordinary environmental designs for the indulgent cat owner.

Here is a smattering of what's available and where to find it.

Litter Boxes

The primary necessity for feline-human cohabitation, the litter box comes in a variety of models with new and improved versions appearing regularly. The litter box, litter and scooper are, the only items you'll need to keep odors contained and the cat receptive to this indoor substitute for its normally out-of-door activity. In addition to the basic box, a tri-paneled screen can be added to enclose the box for cat's privacy and for less scattering of litter.

Furniture and Food

Above and beyond the basic box, there are many advanced designs that offer a cat more privacy and attempt to reduce odors. There are some with cathedral ceilings that can be treated to designer slipcovers so ornamental they would make Mario Buatta proud. They can be made at Pampered Paws, 227 E. 57th St., and other select shops.

Some of the other litter boxes worth examining are Lift 'N Sift, the Dry System, Boodabox, Booda Loo, and "Sweet P" Litter Free System—these and others are available selectively at most pet supply stores.

As for litter, most cats prefer the clay variety, but there are those who favor the cedar or clump style. The litter box—no matter what kind—should be frequently scooped and cleaned. While liners are available, they are not eco-friendly.

Scratching Posts

Cats by nature must stretch and exercise their claws. Therefore, to keep your cat's claws in shape, a scratching board is an absolute necessity. We suggest starting with a simple 30" circular post covered with tough sisal and attached to a heavy square wooden base. One such post is the Felix, which can be ordered from the manufacturer or purchased at your local pet supply store. Other scratching devices are horizontal and some suspend from doorknobs or attach to the right angle of two walls. More elaborate designs include multi-storied buildings in which the cat can play. These bizarre constructions, resembling your cat's native habitat, go by names such as The Ambosoli, The Etosha, and The Zambesi. While extravagant, they reflect only the affection of the cat owners.

Cats prefer a rough surface to scratch and you can never have enough scratching posts and boards to keep your cat's interest. Scratching posts become even more attractive to your cat with the addition of catnip.

Beds

Cats generally prefer to share their person's bed, but occasionally either the cat or the caregiver prefers to have a separate, comfortable location for the cat's play, lounging or private nap. There are as many bedding possibilities for cats as there are for humans, ranging from the popular pillow in a wicker basket to a fleece-lined or pile tunnel bed, a carpeted mailbox, windowsill hammock or fleece-lined teepee.

Furniture and Food

Especially appealing are the overstuffed, miniature foam rubber sofas available in a variety of upholstered covers at Calling all Pets, 301 E. 76th Street. Most special of all is the canopied four-poster bed available at Just Cats, a cat boutique located at 244 E. 60th Street.

Carriers

Inevitably, there will be occasions when you will want to transport your cat either on a short trip in or out of the city or to the veterinarian. Therefore a spacious and airy carrier with a ventilated top is a must. In addition to the traditional box-like carriers, there is the lightweight Sherpa Bag, an excellent and highly recommended carrier that fits safely and comfortably over your shoulder.

Where To Buy

Cat people in New York are fortunate in the number of stores ready to supply their cat's needs. In every neighborhood a good variety of shops offers many different versions of the furnishings you will seek. The following is a selection by location. Cat food is available at every store listed, and unless otherwise indicated, the stores are open seven days. (Annotations are sometimes provided to offer a sense of the nature and scope of supplies available, but not as an evaluation.)

WESTSIDE

LE PET SPA
300 Rector Place
Battery Park City
212-786-9070
Closed Tuesday.
Delivery available.

PETS KITCHEN
116 Christopher Street
212-242-3924
This well-stocked Greenwich Village shop provides delivery and late-hour convenience.

PET'S PALACE
100 West 10th Street
212-727-0525

BEASTY FEAST
237 Bleecker Street
212-243-3261
630 Hudson Street
212-620-7099
Closed Sunday.
Excellent neighborhood centers for cat needs and information. The Hudson Street store has some extraordinary furniture. Delivery available throughout Manhattan.

Furniture and Food

THE BARKING ZOO
172 Ninth Avenue
212-255-0658
238 Third Avenue
212-228-4848
Well stocked stores with a good selection of quality food, toys and furniture. Free local delivery.

THE ANIMAL HOUSE
594 Ninth Avenue
212-757-2924
This shop has all the cat necessities plus a full line of cat food. Free local delivery.

THE PET DEPARTMENT STORE
233 West 54th Street
212-489-9195
A department store indeed, complete with Santa Claus at Christmas. The largest selection of cat furniture in the city and many choices of food, toys and books. This store also places cats for adoption. Delivery available.

CANINE CASTLE FELINE FORTRESS
410 West 56th Street
212-245-1291
Closed Sunday.

INTERNATIONAL KENNEL CLUB
132 West 72nd Street
212-873-6661

PETLAND DISCOUNTS
2675 Broadway
212-222-8851
137 West 72nd Street
212-875-9785

With over 40 locations scattered throughout the five boroughs, you are bound to find one of these deeply stocked chain stores near you.

THE PET MARKET
210 West 72nd Street
212-799-4200

All around service provided in this convenient neighborhood shop. Good variety of cat food, litter boxes, scratching posts and toys. Delivery available.

PET BOWL
440 Amsterdam Avenue
212-595-4200

Offers bonuses for in-store shoppers club and other perks for delivery club. An extensive variety of cat food and furniture is found in this busy emporium.

Furniture and Food

PET STOP
552 Columbus Avenue
212-580-2400
A warm neighborhood center for cat food, furniture, books, toys and valuable advice from the personnel. Discount pet food club and an automatic delivery arrangement.

CREATURE COMFORTS
2778 Broadway
212-864-9964
This is a friendly, well-run, fastidious shop with a well-chosen selection of cat supplies for the Columbia University area. Delivery and grooming available.

LITTLE CREATURES PET FOOD STORES
770 Amsterdam Avenue
212-932-8610
Delivery available.

BEST PETS
1353 St. Nicholas Avenue
212-927-9163

PET CITY
659 West 181st Street
212-740-0088
Delivery available.

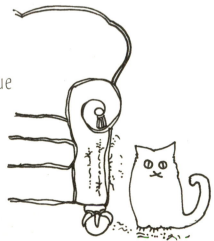

EAST SIDE

PETLAND DISCOUNTS
132 Nassau Street
212-964-1821

THE PET BAR
98 Thompson Street
212-274-0510
A wide array of cat supplies including food and toys. Free delivery.

J.B.J. DISCOUNT PET SHOP
151 East Houston Street
212-982-5310
Closed Sunday.

CREATURE FEATURES
3 Great Jones Street
212-473-5992
Closed Sunday.
Offers extensive information and advice on food and other related items. Delivery available.

LITTLE CREATURES PET FOOD STORES
126 St. Marks Place
212-473-2857
Abundantly stocked shops with a wide range of quality foods, pet medication, furniture and a good toy selection. Delivery available.

Furniture and Food

WHISKERS
235 E. 95th Street
1-800-WHISKERS
This extraordinary pet shop offers a complete range of natural pet foods. Fifteen varieties of cat litter and detailed listings of cat food ingredients are provided in an extensive catalogue. This is a store with a mission and offers valuable suggestions for a healthy cat.

HONEY BUNCH
133 Third Avenue
212-353-2300
Delivery available.

NEW YORK AQUARIUM AND PET SUPPLY
214 East 23rd Street
212-481-7387
Delivery available.

ANIMAL WORLD
219 East 26th Street
212-685-0027
Closed Sunday.
A lively store with a well informed owner and a representative assortment of cat food and accessories. Delivery available.

ANIMAL CRACKERS
159 East 33rd Street

212-725-1970
Delivery available.

THE PETTERY
656 Second Avenue
212-251-0234
Delivery available.

SWEETIE PIE PET SUPPLIES
722 Second Avenue
212-986-4407
Delivery available.

MY PET SHOP
851 Second Avenue
212-682-1635
Closed Sunday.

PETLAND DISCOUNTS
976 Second Avenue
212-755-7228

BEEKMAN PET EMPORIUM
900 First Avenue
212-838-6480

An attractive corner store providing a good selection of cat food and toys, as well as an interesting assortment of cat tchotchkes in pottery and china. Delivery and grooming available.

Furniture and Food

PAMPERED PAWS
227 East 57th Street
212-935-PAWS

The city's most elegant pet shop, appropriate to the neighborhood. The furniture is exceptional, and there is an extensive selection of books and videos. This store also organizes special events, such as birthday parties, for your cat. Quality food plus delivery.

JUST CATS
244 E. 60th Street
212-888-2287

Just as the name says, this unique boutique is devoted entirely to the cat. Almost any cat-related object you can think of can be found here, including an elaborate grand canopied bed.

AMERICAN KENNELS
798 Lexington Avenue
212-838-8460

ANIMAL ATTRACTIONS
335 East 65th Street
212-734-8400
Closed Sunday.
Delivery available.

PET NECESSITIES
236 East 75th Street
212-988-0769
Closed Sunday.
Full line of cat foods and supplies with an extensive assortment of beds. Delivery available.

CALLING ALL PETS
301 East 76th Street
212-249-7387
1590 York Avenue
212-249-PETS
Friendly, efficiently stocked stores with some unusual furniture. An excellent source of local cat information via the busy bulletin board. Delivery available.

MABEL'S
849 Madison Avenue
212-734-3263
One of the city's treasures, this boutique carries a unique selection of clothing (for cats and their companions), housewares, furniture, rugs, art and antiques and much more. (Cat food is not available here.)

PETER'S EMPORIUM FOR PETS
1449 Second Avenue
212-772-3647
This shop is a pleasure to visit. It has an excellent selection of food and accessories. Custom-made wooden beds decorated

with decals and vibrant colors are costly but attractive. The owner generously shares his knowledge with his customers. Delivery available.

KAREN'S FOR PEOPLE AND PETS
1195 Lexington Avenue
212-472-9440
Closed Sunday.
An upscale East Side pet store with an elegant selection of merchandise, unique furniture and food, and a great view of the grooming area. Local delivery is available.

PETLAND DISCOUNTS
304 East 86th Street
212-472-1655

PET SUPERETTE
187 East 93rd Street
212-534-1732
Closed Sunday.
Delivery available.

BROOKLYN

A HUNGRY PET, LTD.
799 Coney Island Avenue
718-856-8100

ACME PET FOOD, INC.
628 Vanderbilt Avenue
718-789-8062
Free local delivery.

ALL FOR PAWS
216 Prospect Park West
718-788-7052
Free delivery.

ANIMAL HOUSE PET FOOD AND GROOMING
2907 Ft. Hamilton Parkway
718-633-3076

ANIMAL PANTRY
697 86th Street
718-680-2220
Delivery available.

NEW YORK PET SUPPLIES
983 63rd Street
718-680-0176
Free delivery.

PET FOOD PLUS
495 King's Highway
718-375-1110

Furniture and Food

QUEENS

NORTHERN PET SUPPLIES
147-32 Northern Blvd., Flushing
1-800-649-PETS
Delivery available.

PET MENU
215-05 Northern Blvd., Bayside
718-224-4PET

PET NOSH
254-07 Northern Blvd., Little Neck
718-229-8976
Delivery available.

BRONX

CITY PETS II
3197 Bainbridge Avenue
914-667-2873
Delivery available.

TRAILER'S TROPICAL PET SHOP
1230 East Gun Hill Road
914-882-2318

NEW JERSEY

CATS & COMPANY, INC.
3 North New York Road, #6
Smithville, NJ 08201
809-748-9449

This boutique in historic Smithville offers clothing, jewelry, gifts and collectibles. (Cat food is not available here.)

LONG ISLAND

CAT LADY ANTIQUES
165 Main Street
Port Washington, LI
516-883-4334

Offers a selection of antique items and collectibles. (Cat food is not available here.)

DELIVERY ONLY

MR. B'S PET DEPOT
718-423-0082

Mr. B's delivers throughout Queens and Manhattan and is willing to beat any price in town. He fills all food requests, and special prescriptions from your vet. This service also delivers bottled water to satisfy the thirsty cat or owner.

WESTSIDE VETERINARY PET
Food Delivery Service
220 West 83 St.
718-423-0082

This is a most accommodating service which stays abreast of all the latest innovations in cat diet-related products.

Beauty Salons

To glamorize your cat, there are services available in a variety of venues; they're particularly appropriate to a long-haired cat. The grooming process includes a bath, claw clipping, a blow dry, and for long hairs the possible "lion cut" or shaving of the cat's fur to resemble its ancestor's mane.

Grooming facilities can be found at some pet shops, veterinarian offices, animal hospitals and specialty shops devoted to the art of beautifying your pet. A number of groomers make house calls, which is much less stressful to your cat, although home services come at a premium price. Appointments are necessary and you should always ask the groomer if he or she will sedate your cat before the beautifying process begins. You can then decide if you think this is an acceptable practice.

Do not be concerned by the number of seemingly dog-oriented groomers, as most tend to cross the species line. Only a few groomers devote their skills solely to cats.

Prices start at about $40 for short-haired cats and $10 more for long-hairs. One groomer prices according to "weight and attitude."

Beauty Salons

WEST SIDE

LE PET SPA
300 Rector Place
212-786-9070

DOG-O-RAMA
161 Seventh Avenue South
212-627-3647

PAWS INN
189 Ninth Avenue
212-645-7297

GROOMING BY JOEY
267 West 25th Street
212-691-0242

ANIMAL HOUSE INC.
594 Ninth Avenue
212-757-2924

PET DEPARTMENT STORE
233 West 54th Street
212-489-9195

CAT-A-COMB
30 West 60th Street
212-262-4529

A CUT ABOVE
207 West 75th Street
212-799-TRIM

YUPPIE PUPPIE PET CARE, INC.
274 West 86th Street
212-877-2747

AMSTERDOG GROOMERS
586 Amsterdam Avenue
212-496-6117

ANITRA CAT GROOMING
309 West 99th Street
212-663-0122

CREATURE COMFORTS
2778 Broadway
212-864-9964

WE KARE KENNELS, INC.
410 West 220th Street
212-567-2100

Beauty Salons

EAST SIDE

CREATURE FEATURES
3 Great Jones Street
212-473-5992

DOGGIE DEAREST
543 East 5th Street
212-254-3204

HONEY BUNCH
133 Third Avenue
212-353-2300

MURRAY HILL ANIMAL HOSPITAL
47 East 30th Street
212-685-2857

EAST BAY ANIMAL CLINIC
612 Second Avenue
212-481-7999

THE PETTERY
656 Second Avenue
212-251-0234

Beauty Salons

EAST SIDE ANIMAL HOSPITAL
321 East 52nd Street
212-751-5176

SUTTON DOG PARLOR
1161 York Avenue
212-355-2850

URSULA LENHARDT
830 Lexington Avenue
212-838-2064

NO STANDING ANYTIME
414 East 73rd Street
212-472-0694

LE CHIEN PET SALON
1461A First Avenue
212-861-8100

KAREN'S
1195 Lexington Avenue
212-472-9440

GROOM AND TAILOR BY REVI
506 East 82nd Street
212-439-0679

Beauty Salons

THE SHAGGY DOG
400 East 88th Street
212-289-0198

PET SUPERETTE AND LAUNDERETTE CORP.
187 East 93rd Street
212-534-1732

HOUSE CALLS ONLY

CAT GROOMING BY HOWARD
212-889-1729

DYANDRIA
212-759-8126
Groomed John Lennon's cat.

Cat Behaviorists

Cat behaviorists, a.k.a. cat psychologists, a.k.a. cat therapists, are the professionals to contact when you can't solve your cat's behavioral problems on your own *and* a check-up has ruled out any medical problem. These cat experts have many years of experience in observing cat behavior and can offer solutions to the cat's problem.

One common problem is the litter box syndrome, which is when the cat decides not to use the litter box in preference to more exposed and less appropriate places. Or your cat may choose not to use the scratching post and opt for your furniture instead. Cats can also develop a sudden antagonism toward another member of the household—either human or animal.

The cat therapist can identify clues the owner may not be able to recognize and provide a solution to these situations so that peace and order can again prevail. Of course, there is not a one hundred percent guarantee, but success is more likely to occur than not.

Cat behaviorists usually work out of veterinarian offices or maintain practices of their own. Some therapists do consultations by phone and are able to solve the problem merely by having the situation described to them. Others prefer to deal with the problem in the cat's home environment or in the veterinarian's office. Listed below are some New York City cat therapists and a selection of books on cat therapy:

ANIMAL BEHAVIOR HOTLINE
212-721-1231

PETER BORCHELT, LINDA GOODLOW, VALIDA SLADE
Animal Behavior Consultants
718-891-4200

PAM JOHNSON, FELINE BEHAVIORIST
Telephone consultations
615-352-5133

BARBARA MEYERS
Holistic Animal Consulting Centre
29 Lyman Avenue, Staten Island
718-720-5555

GAIL DE SCIOSE, CAT COMMUNICATOR
212-831-4666

JOANNA SEERE, SPIRITUAL HEALER

Spiritual healing and counseling for animals that are ill.
212-877-6297

CAROLE C. WILBOURN, CAT THERAPIST AND AUTHOR

Available for house calls and phone consultations (212-741-0397). She will also see your cat by appointment at these two locations:
West Side Veterinary Center
220 West 83rd Street
212-580-1800
The Animal Clinic of New York
1623 First Avenue
212-628-5580

Books & Audio of interest

Eckstein, Warren, **How To Get Your Cat To Do What You Want** (Fawcett)

Johnson, Pam, **Twisted Whiskers: Solving Your Cat's Behavior Problems** (Crossing Press)

Wilbourn, Carole C., **Cat Talk: What Your Cat Is Trying to Tell You** (Contact author at 212-741-0397)

Wilbourn, Carole C., **Cats on the Couch** (Humane Society of New York) All proceeds go to the animals.

Cat Behaviorists

Wilbourn, Carole C., **The Cat Caring Tape** (contact author at 212-741-0397)

Wright, John, C., **Is Your Cat Crazy?** (Macmillan)

Television and Radio

Warren Eckstein appears on Live with Regis and Kathie Lee and hosts the radio program "Pet Show." He has worked with the cats of many celebrities.

When the Owner is Away

Cats are happiest in the places they know best. Therefore, when you go away, it's best for the cat to remain at home. Ask a friend or relative to stay at your house or drop in on your cat. If that's not possible, hire a cat sitter.

Cat Sitters

Cat sitters are unique individuals who will visit your home daily and spend from 20 minutes to an hour doing all the things you would normally do for your cat, including feeding, changing the litter, brushing, playing, and administering any necessary medication. Most sitters will also take in the mail and water your plants. Some sitters will even keep a log of all your cat's activities while you're away. These services are usually about $15 per visit, per cat, with an additional charge for more than one cat. Some sitters will stay overnight should the cat require such attention. (A few sitters prefer to work in their own homes.)

New York sitters have various credentials: some are members of the National Association of Pet Sitters and some may be bonded. References from other satisfied cat owners will direct you to the cat sitters who will set your heart at ease.

When The Owner is Away

Remember to leave the name and number of a back-up sitter, the vet's number, and the phone numbers where you can be reached in case of an emergency.

Some sitters prefer to stay in their own neighborhood but others cover all of Manhattan. The following is a list of cat sitters and cat-sitting services:

ALL OF MANHATTAN

ALL CREATURES GREAT & SMALL PET CARE
212-674-7049

PET CARE NETWORK
212-889-0756

PET PATROL
212-924-6319

PET SITTING
212-791-0122

PUDDLES PET SERVICE
212-410-7338

AMINAH SEEBACH
212-242-7078

URBAN ANIMAL
212-969-8506

DOWNTOWN

CAT CARE BY BARBARA
212-929-5372

JUDY DUFFY
212-966-1852

PET AND PLANT CARE
212-349-0244

ROYAL MAJESTY FELINE SERVICE
212-598-0018

TENDER LOVING PET CARE
212-989-6710

EAST SIDE

PATTI ADJAMINE
212-427-8273

SHIRLEY APPELSON
212-982-6379

When The Owner is Away

CAT CARE-EAST
212-838-2996

CHRISTIAN
212-535-6724

KATIA GROSSMAN
212-734-0052

LOTSALUV PET CARE SERVICE
212-980-8088

PERFECT PET CARE
212-686-3937

PURRFECT CAT CARE
212-362-2175

WEST SIDE

CAT CARE WEST
212-947-6190

PURRFECT CAT CARE
212-362-2175

YVETTE NABEL
212-535-6937

Veterinary Boarding

Boarding your cat should be your last resort and considered only if your cat needs special medication or frequent treatment. Below is a select list of Manhattan veterinary boarding places, downtown to uptown.

EAST VILLAGE VETERINARIAN
241 Eldridge
212-674-8640

ST. MARKS VETERINARY HOSPITAL
348 E. 9th Street
212-477-2688

VILLAGE VETERINARIAN
204 E. 10th Street
212-979-9870

THE CAT PRACTICE
137 5th Avenue
212-677-1401

RICHARD NOVICK
267 W. 25th Street
212-691-9270

When The Owner is Away

CHELSEA DOG AND CAT HOSPITAL
303 W. 20th Street
212-929-6963

FABULOUS FELINES
657 Second Avenue
212-889-9865

EAST SIDE ANIMAL HOSPITAL
321 E. 52nd Street
212-751-5176

NEW YORK VETERINARY HOSPITAL
301 E. 55th Street
212-355-5490

ANIMAL MEDICAL CENTER
510 E. 62nd Street
212-838-8100

PARK EAST ANIMAL HOSPITAL
52 E. 64th Street
212-832-8417

UNIVERSITY ANIMAL HOSPITAL
354 E. 66th Street
212-288-8884

ANSONIA VETERINARY HOSPITAL
207 W. 75th Street
212-496-2100

FELINE HEALTH
1533 First Avenue
212-879-0700

MERCY VETERINARY HOSPITAL
134 E. 82nd Street
212-861-5601

YORKVILLE ANIMAL HOSPITAL
227 E. 84th Street
212-249-8802

WESTSIDE VETERINARY CENTER
220 W. 83rd Street
212-580-1800

WEST PARC VETERINARY CLINIC
8 W. 86th Street
212-362-9100

ANIMAL GENERAL
692 Columbus Avenue
212-222-4700

When The Owner is Away

COLUMBIA ANIMAL HOSPITAL
229 W. 101st Street
212-864-1144

145TH STREET ANIMAL HOSPITAL
454 W. 145th Street
212-234-3489

Travel

Cats are primarily homebodies, but there are owners on the move who wish or need to travel with their cat. For them, the principal issues become the method of transportation and the cooperation of the carrier.

It is simplest to travel with a cat in a light-weight over the shoulder bag such as the Sherpa, or in a ventilated, light-weight, traditional carrier.

The small size of cats makes it easy to take them on trains, taxis, and buses. The farther away you get from home, the more complicated the arrangements.

A token for your cat is not required on the MTA subway or bus, just a willing driver. Cats, however, are not allowed on Amtrak or Greyhound.

These local lines allow cats on board:

LONG ISLAND RAILROAD
718-217-5477
Your cat must be in a carrying case.

Travel

PATH
800-234-7284

Cats in carrying cases only are welcome.

METRO-NORTH COMMUTER RAILROAD
212-532-4900

Cats are acceptable in a carrier, though the conductor makes all final decisions.

NEW JERSEY TRANSIT
201-762-5100

Cats in carriers only allowed on these buses.

HAMPTON JITNEY
800-936-0440

Cats permitted in carrying cases at a $10 charge each way.

Air Travel

Flying your cat is a risky business. If you are determined to have your cat with you, call your airline immediately and try to arrange for the cat to travel with you in the passenger cabin. Only one animal is allowed in coach and one in first class, so reserve early. Your cat will have to be in either a carrier provided by the airline (which fits under the seat) or the Sherpa bag. Horror stories about animals shipped with the cargo, loose in the hold, and lost for several weeks while the plane continued its international itinerary are enough to turn any cat owner's hair gray and may dissuade you from flying with your cat.

If you must take your cat with you, the following sources might be of help:

WORLD WIDE PET TRANSPORT
718-539-5543

This outfit handles all the hassles of international and domestic travel that involve the transportation of a cat. They also arrange for surface transport within a 200 mile radius of most major U.S. airports.

Barish, Eileen, **Vacation with Your Pet** (Pet Friendly Publications), 1994

Places likely to welcome you and your pet.

"TRAVELING WITH TOWSER"
Quaker Professional
TWT, Dept. PGP 585
Hawthorne Court
Galesburg, IL. 61401

Provides a list of accommodations for cats.

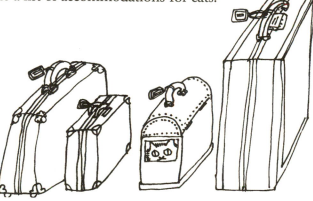

Special Events

Housebound cats are not the most likely guests at public events, but there are a few where they are very welcome and their owners will be delighted to be involved.

St. Francis of Assisi's feast day is October 4, and is celebrated with a Blessing of the Animals service at a number of Catholic and Episcopal churches. We've listed a few, but also check neighborhood churches for additional events.

THE BLESSING OF THE ANIMALS
Cathedral of St. John The Divine
West 112th Street and Amsterdam Avenue
212-316-7400
An especially wonderful service. Cats are allowed in their carriers, on leashes or in the arms of their owners. A carrier is recommended.

ST. LUKE'S IN THE FIELDS
Hudson and Christopher Street
212-924-0562

THE BLESSING OF THE ANIMALS
Prospect Park
718-965-8965
All animals are invited.

CENTRAL PRESBYTERIAN CHURCH
64th Street and Park Avenue
212-838-0808

All animals are invited to a splendid traditional Christmas Eve service during which there is a blessing of the animals.

INCATS INTERNATIONAL CAT SHOW
Madison Square Garden
33rd Street and 7th Avenue
718-855-1928

Held every year over the first weekend of March. This world class competition includes everything and anything about cats. There are lectures on the latest developments in cat care, health, nutrition, genetics and behavior, a feline shopping mall with hundreds of products, new breeds on exhibition at the Breed Information Center, and the Iams Company "Walk In" super cat contest for shelter-rescued cats.

Schedules for other local cat shows are listed in *Cat Fancy* magazine.

The Cat as Art

A special pleasure for cat owners is seeing their cat's image captured in some memorable pose by an artist or photographer. Some very talented artists have devoted their careers to cat portraits. Photography, sculpture, as well as oil, watercolor and pastel paintings are available by commission—take your pick. These portraits are usually framed, but often find their way onto holiday cards, note paper, and tee shirts as well.

ANIMAL ANGEL
P.O. Box 03712
Elmont, NY 11003

Renderings done from snapshots. Send a SASE for information.

JUDITH GWYN BROWN
522 East 85th Street
212-288-1599

This children's book illustrator specializes in cat portraits. She will paint a cat alone or with its owner, and she works from both photos and observation. Her watercolors and oils are painted in both realistic and imaginary settings, from the living room couch to fantasy environments. Watercolors are $600 for a 14 x 17 portrait; oils start at $1,000 for the same size.

CAT ATTRACTIONS
P.O. Box 404
Merrick, NY 11566

Portrait sculpture rendered from a color photo. Prices start at about $85.

FUR FACES
155 Bank Street
Studio 516D
New York, NY 10014
212-929-2430

Theresa Cannon-King and Nym Bjorkland photograph your cat at home. The minimum cost is $250 and prices for various size prints range from $80 to $125.

PET PORTRAITS BY DOROTHY FRANCES GOLDSTEIN
212-825-0168

This photographer works only in the animal's home in order to see the cat at its most natural in its own surroundings.

S. G. HOFFMAN
42 Gabriel Road
Cochecton, New York 12726
914-583-6315

Ceramic sculptures created from several photos are combined with the cat's name. The models are hand sculpted, painted and mounted on a wooden base. Sculptures are seven inches high and the starting price is $50.

JOAN'S NEEDLECRAFT STUDIO
240 E. 29th Street
New York, NY
212-532-7129

Bring a photo of your cat here and have that portrait of your cat painted onto a needlepoint canvas. The price is $125 for one cat, $150 for two on a single canvas. For an additional fee, the needlepoint can be done for you by artists in Haiti.

PORTRAITS BY DEBRA HOPE
794 Bear Hill Road
Berwyn, PA 19312
610-647-3443

This painter does portraits in oil. She prefers to take her own photos of your cat in your home, and then paint from the photos. Depending on size, costs range from $350 to $2,000.

PETOGRAPHY
25 Central Park West, Suite 3A
New York, NY
212-245-0914

Jim Dratfield and Paul Conglin photograph your cat at home or in their studio. They work in both sepia and black and white. Prices for one framed and two matted photos are $325, $25 of which goes to an animal cause of your choice. They also make postcards and notecards.

PORTRAITS BY LILA PRITCHARD
212-691-1460

Pastels made from photos cost $85 with an additional $35 if the sitting is done in the home. The drawing takes from three to five weeks and includes the full figure of your cat.

PAULETTE SINCLAIR
60 West 8th Street
New York, NY 10003
212-533-4208

Your cat can sit for this photographer at home or in her studio. Prices start at $120.

PRISCILLA SNYDER
212-344-2209

Your cat's image is embroidered in the fabric of unusual custom-made totebags. The tote's handle is designed to look like a tail. Priscilla also makes life-like cloth sculptures.

The Cat as Art

TARA STEVENS
9 East Main Street
Pawling, NY
212-929-2992

A photographer who visits your cat at home. She can put your cat's picture on tee shirts, pillowcases and tote bags.

ALICE SU
321 East 22nd Street
212-477-0977

Widely published feline photographer specializing in at-home portraits.

MIMI VANG OLSEN
545 Hudson Street
212-675-5410

Mimi Vang Olsen is a world-famous portrait painter who has her own gallery in Greenwich Village. She does commissioned portraits of cats, first visiting your cat at home, taking photos there, and then painting the final portrait in her gallery, surrounded by her own four cats. Prices start at $2,500 for one cat; additional cats are $500 each.

Write Aways

Extraordinary cat paraphernalia, supplies and necessities are available through mail order catalogs. Write away and receive wonderful browsing materials filled with ideas and ways to entertain your cat, enhance his or her health and environment, and make both of your lives infinitely more fun.

CATS, CATS & MORE CATS
P.O. Box 270
Monroe, NY 10950
914-782-4141

CAT CLAWS
P.O. Box 1001
Morrilton, AK 72110
800-783-0977

THE CAT'S MEOW
Box 8826
Cincinnati, OH 45208
"Cool cat stuff" and great cat-related gifts.

CITY MARKET
310 West St. Julene Street
Savannah, GA 41401
912-236-CATS

CRAZY CAT LADY
P.O. Box 691920
Los Angeles, CA 90069
213-782-0490
Kitty crowns and thrones as well as more practical accessories.

DIRECT BOOK SOURCE
P.O. Box 3073 CM
Wenatchee, WA 98807
Free cat book catalog.

FELIX
3623 Fremont Avenue North
Seattle, WA 98103
Free catalog of quality books and supplies.

HOLISTIC PET CENTER
15599 SE 2nd Drive
Clackamas, OR 97015
Health food for pets.

KENSINGTON CAT COMPANY
39 Dodge Street, Suite 249
Beverly, MA 01915-1705

800-772-6615

Uncommon products for discriminating cat lovers. Free gifts with every order.

MAIL ORDER PET SHOP

250 W. Executive Drive
Edgewood, NY 11717
1-800-366-7387

Full line of pet supplies.

KITTY KRAFTS

Fine Arts by Lauralynn
60 Evelyn Terrace
Wayne, NJ 07470
201-696-7064

Victorian kitty baskets, cross-stitch portraits and wooden door stops of your very own cat.

MORRELL'S NEW DIRECTIONS NATURE PET CARE CATALOG

P.O. Box 30
Orient, ME 04471

A natural alternative cat care catalog.

NEUTRON INDUSTRIES

2801 Spring Grove Avenue
Cincinnati, OH 45225
800-421-8481

Offers environmentally safe, biodegradable deodorizers.

PEDIGREES
1989 Transit Way
Box 905
Brockport, NY 14420-0905
1-800-548-4786

Grooming gloves with a textured surface to stimulate your cat's coat and skin, special dental kits to bring your cat's teeth up to hygienic snuff, and toy snowmen filled with catnip. Obviously something for every kitty.

WHISKERS
235 East 9th Street
New York, NY 10003
800-WHISKERS

Alternative pet health care offering natural foods. They provide a list of ingredients for most of the canned and dry foods they offer. Also fifteen varieties of cat litter are available. This store and catalog are a must for the serious cat owner.

Good Reading and Viewing

Books

Cats love to come between you and the book you are reading, although they really shouldn't interfere if the subject is feline. The available cat literature is wide-ranging; what follows is only a sampling of what is in print and available. (For books specifically about behavior problems, see pages 55 and 56, and for vacation guides, see page 67.)

Alderton, David, **Eyewitness Handbook of Cats** (Dorling-Kindersley), 1994

Amory, Cleveland, **The Best Cat Ever** (Little Brown), 1993

Behrind, Katrina and Wigler, Monica **The Complete Book of Cat Care** (Barrons), 1991

Carlson, Delbert, **Cat Owners Home Veterinary Handbook** (Howell House), 1983

Good Reading and Viewing

Carus, Roger, **Harper Illustrated Handbook of Cats** (Harper)
An excellent guide to all the breeds.

Curtis, Patricia, **The Indoor Cat** (Perigee), 1981
Specially applicable to living in New York.

Edney, Andrew, **ASPCA Complete Cat Care Manual** (Dorling-Kindersley), 1992

Eldridge, Wayne, **Best Pet Name Book Ever** (Barrons), 1990
Couch Potato, Chainsaw, Guacamole, Zinfandel, for example.

Fogle, Bruce, **101 Questions Your Cat Would Ask Its Vet if Your Cat Could Talk** (Carrol and Graf), 1993

Good Reading and Viewing

Frazier, Anitra, **The New Natural Cat** (Plume), 1990
Treating your cat holistically.

Kunkel, Paul, **How to Toilet Train Your Cat** (Workman), 1991

McGinnis, **The Well Cat Book** (Random House), 1995

Maggetti, Phil, **Guide to a Well Behaved Cat** (Barrons), 1995

Riddle, Roz, **The City Cat** (Fawcett Crest), 1987
The city is New York and the writer an owner of Fabulous Felines.

Siegel, Mordecai, **Cornell Book of Cats** (Villard), 1989
A classic overview of cat health and behavior.

Taylor, David, **The Ultimate Cat Book** (Simon & Schuster), 1989

Taylor, David, **You and Your Cat** (Knopf), 1986

Thomas, Elizabeth Marshall, **Tribe of Tiger** (Simon & Schuster), 1994

Treselor, Liz, **Cat Horoscope Book** (Dorchester), 1982

Good Reading and Viewing

Wennirstrom, Genia, **Cat Horoscopes** (Abrams), 1992
Supposedly for each of your cat's nine lives.

Wolff, H.G., **Your Healthy Cat: Homeopathic Medicines for Common Feline Ailments** (North Atlantic Books), 1991

Videos

Sometimes practical information comes from watching rather than reading. Almost all videos on pets are instructional and especially helpful for the new cat owner. Videos offer a wonderful opportunity to survey the variety and behavior of most available types. Videos can be bought in pet stores and occasionally rented from video stores.

Cat Pet Care, Ted 3133
Everything cat lovers ever wanted to know about their beloved cat and more.

Cat Care, Dr. Michael Fox Animal Series, Maier TMG102

Cats—Finicky Facts and Entertaining Tails, TBS Productions

Feline, ASPCA Inc.

Kittens to Cats, Video Pet Series

Good Reading and Viewing

Longhaired Cat Breeds, Viacom Productions

Non-Stop Kittens, Pet Avision Inc.

Photographing Pets, Imaginwerks 800-882-1679

Shorthaired Cat Breeds, Viacom Productions

Toilet Training Your Pet, Smart Cat Productions

Video Catnip, Pet Avision, Inc.
This one is solely for your cat's pleasure. Endless birds and small animals to whet your indoor cat's appetite for the great outdoors.

Magazines

Read these for fun and for keeping up to date on the latest cat news, products, photography and book reviews.

Advocate (Animal Protection News)
American Humane Association
63 Inverness Drive East
Englewood, CO 80112
Animal welfare and protection, pet care information.

American Cat Fanciers Association Yearbook
Box 203, Point Lookout, MO 65726
Articles on cats and year-end awards.

Good Reading and Viewing

ASPCA Bulletin
ASPCA
441 E. 92nd Street
New York, NY 10128
Deals with animal issues, pet care, news and reviews.

Bide-A-Wee News
Bide-A-Wee Home Association
410 E. 38th Street
New York, NY 10016
Articles on this association's activities and tips on animal care.

Cat Fanciers Almanac
Cat Fanciers Association
1805 Atlantic Avenue
Manasquan, NJ 08736
Calendar of cat shows, veterinary news, breed articles. Important annual for all cat enthusiasts.

Cat Fancy
2401 Beverly Blvd.
Los Angeles, CA 90057
Official Cat Lovers of America magazine—advice on health, behavior, breeds. Edited for cat and kitten enthusiasts, caregivers and professional breeders.

Cats Magazine
Box 290037
Port Orange, FL 32129

Professional information and advice on care and health topics, as well as articles on cats in art, history, literature and culture.

Cat Talk
Cat Collectors
33161 Wendy Drive
Sterling Heights, MI 48310

Catalogue of new and antique cat porcelains and figurines.

Cat World International
Box 35635
Phoenix, AZ 85069

Serves the interests of serious owners and breeders.

I Love Cats
Grass Roots Publishing
950 Third Avenue
New York, NY 10022

Contains articles frequently written by cat owners and covers only household cats.

Natural Pet: Alternative Lifestyles for All Companion Animals
National Animal Health Alliance
Pet Publications
P.O. Box 351
Trilby, FL 33593

Naturalistic approach to animal health and lifestyle.

Good Reading and Viewing

Perspectives on Cats
Cornell Feline Health Center
College of Veterinary Medicine
Cornell University
Ithaca, NY 14853

Provides practical feline health care tips for cat caregivers.

Pet Focus
1 Kimback Court
Dermvet Inc.
West Caldwell, NJ 07006

Provides pet health information for cat owners.

Pet Gazette
1309 N. Halifax
Daytona Beach, FL 32118

For animal lovers.

Pethouse
215 Lexington Avenue
New York, NY 10016

Available via New York City pet stores. Filled with information and local ads.

Pet Partners
Delta Society
Box 1080
Renton, WA 98057

Animal-assisted activities and pet therapy.

Happy Hunting Grounds

The Guinness Book of Records tells us a cat has been known to live to 36 years but the norm is about half of that and sometimes less. Parting with a beloved pet is a very painful experience, especially when its owner must make the decision to have its life ended. Whatever the cause of death, the loss is major and help in dealing with bereavement is often needed. For bereavement counseling the following sources for help are available.

ANIMAL CLINIC OF NEW YORK
1623 First Avenue
212-628-5580
Carole C. Wilbourn provides grief therapy and counsel for people and surviving cats by appointment only. She also makes house calls and can be contacted at 212-741-0397.

ASPCA
424 E. 92nd Street
212-876-7700
Paula Anreder, grief counselor.

BIDE-A-WEE
410 E. 38th Street
212-532-6395

Muriel Franzblau, grief counselor.

BIDE-A-WEE
Wantagh Shelter
118 Old Country Road, Westhampton
516-785-4199

Wendy Grossman, Director of Bereavement Services.

HOLISTIC ANIMAL CONSULTING CENTRE
29 Lyman Avenue
Staten Island, NY 10305
718-720-5548

Grief therapist, Barbara Meyers.

WEST SIDE VETERINARY CENTER
220 West 83rd Street
212-580-1800
Carole C. Wilbourn provides grief therapy and counsel by appointment.

Pet Cemeteries and Crematories

The knowledge that the cat's remains have been suitably cared for is a substantial comfort in dealing with loss. Pet cemeteries and crematories are located in various suburban communities in Westchester, Nassau and Sussex Counties, and New Jersey. Here is a sampling of the most accessible sites.

NEW JERSEY

BERGEN HUDSON PET MORTUARY
351 Palisade Avenue
Cliffside Park, NJ 07010
201-941-1314
This is actually the area office for the Abingdon Hill Pet Cemetery in Montgomery, NY. The 52-acre site offers pick-up, cremation and burial. Burial costs start at $100 and go up to $500 for casket and burial. Cremation costs, including urn, start at $165.

ABBEY GLEN PET MEMORIAL PARK
187 Route 94, Lafayette, NJ 07848
800-972-3118

This 75-acre site contains 14 acres of cemetery. Costs for cremation or burial start at $90. Burial charges rise to $400 including casket. Pick-up is an additional charge.

NEW YORK

ABINGDON HILL PET CEMETERY
148 Youngblood Road
Montgomery, NY 12549
914-361-2200

(See Bergen Hudson Pet Mortuary above)
This unusual location is beautifully landscaped and is always open. Owners have the rare opportunity to have their own ashes laid to rest with those of their pets.

ALDSTATE PET CREMATION
306 83rd Street
Brooklyn, NY 718-745-2104

Pick-ups for cremation are made in all boroughs. Costs begin at $130.

HARTSDALE CANINE CEMETERY (ALSO KNOWN AS HARTSDALE PET CEMETERY)
75 North Central Avenue
Hartsdale, NY 10530
914-949-2583

Despite the name, cats too can make this their final resting place. Hartsdale has been in operation since 1896 and is the oldest pet cemetery in the United States. Special events are held to commemorate the deceased animals. Cost of burial is about $500 (depending on choice of casket); cremation is $150. Pick up service available.

SHELTERVALE PET CEMETERY
33 Warner Road
Huntington, NY 11743
516-362-8770

In operation since 1927. The charge for plot and burial is $385, and casket costs range from $35 to $150.

Organizations

There are several opportunities in New York where cat lovers can share their genuine concern and love for felines and bring pleasure and solace to others.

ANIMAL LOVER'S INTERACTION
P.O. Box 399
Stuyvesant Station
New York, NY 10009
212-721-4664

An organization for those who want to share their interest and enthusiasm for animals with other pet lovers.

DELTA SOCIETY
c/o Colgate-Palmolive Company
300 Park Avenue
New York, NY 10022
212-310-2802

Seeks to create new partnerships between people and animals and shows how animals improve human health and well-being, helps owners deal with the loss of a pet, and trains volunteers to visit hospitals, nursing homes and schools with their pets.

NEW YORKERS FOR COMPANION ANIMALS
1324 Lexington Avenue, #2
New York, NY 10128
212-427-8273

A rescue, adoption and advocacy operation for abandoned cats. Works to place adult animals in welcoming homes.

POWARS (PET OWNERS WITH AIDS RESOURCE SERVICES)
P.O. Box 1116
Madison Square Station, NY 10159
212-744-0842

This group offers help caring for a cat to people with AIDS.

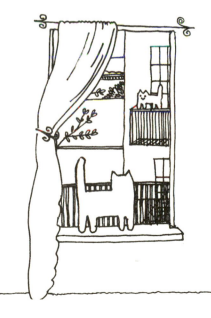

Info at Your Fingertips

Emergency Numbers

ANIMAL MEDICAL CENTER
212-838-8100
Emergency vet service at all hours.

ASPCA
212-722-3620
Receives lost cats. A very small percentage of missing cats are, in fact, ever located.

MANHATTAN VETERINARY GROUP
212-988-1000, Open until 1:00 a.m.

NATIONAL ANIMAL POISON CONTROL CENTER
800-548-2423
Available 365 days a year, this twenty-four hour emergency hotline offers veterinary consultation. Fee is $30.

PET LINE
800-564-5704
A computerized service registering cats lost and found.

Odds and Ends

The following miscellany brings practical and sometimes unusual and unexpected information to you and your cat.

FRIENDS OF ANIMALS
800-321-PETS

Referrals to veterinarians for neutering and spaying at reduced rates.

HELEN W. HARTIG AND MADDY TARNOFSKY, ATTORNEYS-AT-LAW
200 W. 54th Street
New York, NY 10019
212-757-8080

Specialists in tenant representation involving pet-related issues.

KARIN'S IN THE KITCHEN
212-472-1618

Offers tasty cat cookies for people and irresistible toys for cats.

PET LOVERS HELPLINE
900-776-0007

A helpline service for such diverse problems as hairballs, fleas, and bad breath.

PENNY'S CATNIP PILLOWS FOR CATS AND POTPOURRI PILLOWS FOR PEOPLE
271 Pine Ave.
Mays Landing, NJ 08330

PET TAXI
227 East 56th St.
212-755-6000
Ready to take your cat from doorstep to doorstep anywhere in the city (with or without owner).

The following will give you insight into your cat's life—or next life.

ANIMAL PSYCHICS
900-680-0505, ext. 565
Offers to tell you what your cat is thinking. Telephone readings will put you in touch with your cat. However, you must be 18 or over. $2.98 per minute.

LYDIA HIBY
909-789-0330
Insights into your cat's psyche. Monday and Tuesday only. $25 for 15 minutes per cat.

Afterword

The warm presence of a loyal and loving cat with its frolic-some behavior is a fascination from which we never tire. However, to be worthy of such loyalty one must be an attentive and responsible caretaker. We hope the information in this book helps you to do just that and that you will make use of the people, places, and services New York provides to make your cat's life healthy and fulfilled.

About the Author

Bill Dworkin shares his New York apartment with two cats, Sylvia and Jake. A former marketing executive at Rizzoli and Harry N. Abrams, he is convinced that cats are as beautiful and fascinating as works of art.

About the Editor

Carole C. Wilbourn is a New York based cat therapist. She co-founded the first veterinary hospital in New York City exclusively devoted to cats and has written four books on cat behavior. She also writes a monthly column for *Cat Fancy* magazine.

About the Illustrator

Joy Sikorski is the author-illustrator of *How to Draw a Radish,* to be published by Chronicle Books in late 1995.